SONSHINE AND SHADOWS

A Lifetime of Poems

Revised and Expanded

by Lynn B. Fowler

This collection is © copyright Lynn B. Fowler 2015. All rights reserved. Apart from small excerpts for purposes of review or publicity, no part of this collection may be reproduced by any means without explicit written permission from the author.
Some individual poems have been published in various magazines under the names Lynn Smith or Lynn Cox.

Published in Australia by King of Glory Ministries International under the imprint KOGMI Books

Paperback edition first published 2015
by Birdcatcher Books
Hardcover edition first published 2017
by Birdcatcher Books

If you enjoy and are blessed by this book, please help others to find it by leaving a review on your favourite online book store or, if you have a web site, on your site.

ISBN 978-1-7635737-0-3

DEDICATION

*This book is dedicated to
my Saviour and King
the Lord Jesus Christ*

CONTENTS

Poem	**Page**
Revelation	7
Memory	10
No Comfortable Walk	12
Old Woman in a Home	14
The Artist	15
The Elephant Years	16
The Soldier's Song	18
Sad Houses	20
Agapé	22
But Yesterday	23
Christmas Conversations	24
Deserted Wife	26
Awakening	28
Night of Fright	29
Don't Ask Me to Be Yesterday	30
Morning City Far Away	32
Peter	33
Winter Hope	36
For Brian	37
The Hermit	38
Goodbye	40
Day Before Pension	42
Look at Christmas	44
Whom Shall I Follow?	46
The Doll	48
Waiting	50
God is So Stubborn	52
Harsh Words	54

CONTENTS Continued

Poem	Page
Old Houses	55
Aftermath	56
Defining the Infinite	58
First Love	60
Calvary	62
Dewdrop	63
Incredible love	64
The Disposable Man	66
The Spirit of Xmas	68
The Offering	70
Like Sweetest Grapes	71
George	72
For Me	74
Ask Not	76
Marc	77
Full Circle	78
Decision	80
July Morning	82
No God?	84
An End	86
Galatians 2:20	87
Five Loaves	88
Surrender	90
Desolation	92
Jack	93
Nature's Triumph	94
Farewell	95
Substitute	96

CONTENTS Continued

Poem	Page
The Photo	100
Not a Poem	102
By Jesus' Blood	104
Sure of Christ's Love	105
Lost	106
Incarnate	108
Hour of Triumph	110
O Lord You Stand Alone	111
War in Heaven	113
Beyond Imagination	115

INTRODUCTION

This collection represents fifty years of expressing my thoughts and feelings through the medium of poetry. Much of it relates directly to my life: my joys and sorrows, struggles and triumphs, friends and family. Some is based on my observation of the lives of others, and my thoughts about life in general, or my responses to articles in the media. Some expresses simple delights; some deep theological or philosophical ponderings.

Through it all runs the theme of my relationship with the Lord Jesus Christ. My faith in Him is the defining parameter of my life, the filter through which all else must pass. Hence the title of this collection is "Sonshine and Shadows" - not a spelling mistake, but a reference to the Son of God and the light He sheds upon everything. I have, however, included a few of my very early poems, written before I came to know Jesus as my personal Lord and Saviour. I wonder if you will be able to pick them out?

As well as a variety of subjects, the poems in this collection cover a range of styles, from traditional to modern with one or two experimental ones, and vary in length from a few lines to several pages.

With so many variables, deciding on the order in which the poems should be offered presented something of a challenge. Should I group them according to subject? Would it be better to place them in date order - and if so should it run forward from the earliest poems or backward from the most recent? Should I take the easy way out and simply put the poems in alphabetical order?

In the end I settled on an arrangement which allows most poems to be read at a single opening of a page, so that a two-page poem will begin on the left hand page and finish on the right.

The purpose of poetry is to touch the heart, not just the mind, and my prayer is that these poems will touch your heart. I pray that some will speak to your own struggles, conflicts and delights, and perhaps offer some understanding; that some will challenge you about the sad realities of the world in which we live; and that some will create in you a growing hunger for an ever-deepening relationship with the King of the universe.

Lynn B. Fowler
Victoria, Australia
October 2015

REVELATION

(Revelation 1:12-17)

I knew You
my friend
together trudging
dust-heavy roads
together sharing
the joys and burdens
of our souls.

I followed You
my rabbi:
teacher unlike any other
dissecting the wisdom
of the ages
with scalpel-words.

I watched You
miracle-worker
touching blindness with sight
touching lack with abundance
touching death
with life.

***

***

I glimpsed You
in Your majesty
as on the mountain briefly
suppressed glory sundered humanity
and breaking forth
dazzled us
with light.

I leaned against You
dearly loved
at that strange-sad supper
where You took a servant's towel
and served us
not with bread and wine
but with Yourself.

I stood by You
in Your brokenness:
watched helplessly
as they beat You,
mocked You,
pierced You
and left You
to death's agonies
with criminals.

***

***
I welcomed You
risen conqueror
as leaving death's
invalid chains behind
and bursting forth
You walked among us
in victory.

But now...

I see
with eyes newly opened
One I never knew:
fire-blazing eyes
and furnaced-bronze feet;
once oft-heard voice roars
like all the oceans of the world;
once child-holding hands
hold stars;
once familiar face
outshines the sun.

Now
I understand
My God and King
why ancients said
that looking on Your face
one could not live:
and I fall at Your feet
as dead.

MEMORY

Your photo slips
from some dusty
and long-forgotten
volume, and I
search that firm
but loving face
for something
that will fit
my memory.
Try as I may
I cannot
sweep away
the misting years.
The days
of our shared
lives have shut
their doors:
and I
cannot see inside
to what was there;
and though
the warmth remains
the fires
that gave it birth
have long been

***

***
buried in the dust
of time.
Your photo
tells me nothing:
for your photo
is not you
but only
a shadow
whose substance
has long since
slipped away.

NO COMFORTABLE WALK

No comfortable
easy walk
but just
hard roads
and dirty feet.
Dust.
Flies.
Sweat.
Not nice, clean,
sanitary types,
but lepers
and demoniacs.
No high-brow intellectuals
of sensitive understanding,
but coarse and common folk -
tax collectors,
fishermen,
and prostitutes.
You met them where they were,
touched them
with Yourself.
The dregs of society
but You
didn't see them that way.
They're still around

***

***
still needing all You are.
And I long
to walk where You have walked
to touch them with Your love -
so, Lord, how come
my life is so
infuriatingly
middle class?

OLD WOMAN IN A HOME

She sat rocking
tired eyes searching,
hopeful, for visitors,
though she knew none would come.
The grey mists of days
swirled about her
till past and present merged.
She had seen lovers,
friends, come and go:
now non remained.
Had watched
her gay fair-haired
youth fade to sad
grey-haired oblivion
as the greased years
slipped from her grasp.
And now, alone
in winter's memory
of springtime sun,
she rocked.

THE ARTIST

He mixes his tints
with age-learned patience
blending the hues with tenderness
that Nature might envy.
His brushes
extensions of himself
caress the canvas;
his measured strokes
cover the white
with the colours of his soul
and shape on it
the image, not of what he paints,
but of himself.

THE ELEPHANT YEARS

Remember
when we were small
and the years
were elephants
huge and cumbersome
plodding ponderously past
filling our world
with sight, and smell, and sound,
and stretching our moments
to their limits
giving us room
to explore each new experience
and time
to savour every strange excitement?
But wild, impatient youth
did not want elephants -
it longed instead
to ride the wild gazelle
and race the wind …

***

***

... and now
we are no longer small
and the years
are dragonflies
flitting silently -
and often unnoticed -
from our grasp:
darting by
before we have time
to know them.
Changing
changing
and gone
even as we watch.
And sometimes
in the wing-beat of a moment
I look back
and wish
that once again
the years
were elephants.

THE SOLDIER'S SONG

(Matthew 27:54)

(It is finished!)...
Is it really finished?
    Is it all over?
        Is it really finished?
or has it only just begun?

Have they really killed You?
    Are You really dead now?
        Soon to be forgotten?
Or are You like
the setting sun
    which comes again
        which lives again
tomorrow?

Will they be content now
to see You dead and buried?
Will Your words all fade now?
Your wonders be forgotten?
And all the things
    You said and did
will they be buried in Your grave?

                        ***

***
Have we found the answer?
      The way to quiet the whispers?
Can things get back to normal?
Or have we unleashed a force
      that will not end?
           that will destroy us?
What have we done?
      What have we done?
I fear that we have crucified ...
                God's Son!

SAD HOUSES

Sad houses
standing naked
their lace and finery
long ago
stripped away;
they lean blindly
together
their eyes put out
and patched
with warped and
rotting boards
swinging creakily
from rusty nails.
Above
the crumbling facade
charred beams
stand stark against
the winter sky,
shattered skeletons
of once-loved glory
now forsaken
by all
save the sparrows
and mice.

***

***
Sad houses
dying ungracefully -
ashes
       to ashes
              and dust ...

AGAPÉ

(1 Corinthians 13:1-3)

Although my voice may speak with words
from all the earth, and heaven above,
its sound is but a futile din
unless the breath behind is love.

And I may see the days ahead
and plumb God's deepest mysteries,
and seeing all, be darkness yet
unless His love sees through my eyes.

Or I may stand as firm as rock
with faith to make the mountain move
yet find my faith is desolate
unless the moving force is love.

Yes, even if I give away
all that I have, then die for Him,
all sacrifice is self-deceit
unless His love has lived within.

Love is patient, love is kind
Love does not seek its own way
Love always hopes, always believes:
Love never fails.

BUT YESTERDAY

But yesterday
I climbed the apple tree
and stood above the world
and felt the warmth
of springtime sun
and marvelled
at the joy of being young.
But yesterday
I ran through tall brown grass
and stopped beside a creek
and broke
its shining mirror surface with a stone
and wondered
at the ripples all around.
But yesterday
I watched a swallow fly
far, far beyond the cloud.
Fifty years?
No, that I can't believe.
It seems
no more than yesterday to me.

CHRISTMAS CONVERSATIONS

Have you heard the rumour?
Mary's with child!
and her not married, you know!
Shame! What's the world coming to?
Once they would have stoned
such a hussy
but now
she just gets married quietly
and hopes people can't count.

You say you want a room, sir?
You've got to be joking!
You should have booked a year ago.
Bethlehem's crawling with people
(or hadn't you noticed?)
and after all we are the only inn.
What's that? Your wife's having a child?
So what!
Birth is a natural process, you know.
Well, if you insist, there is the cattle shed.
Anything to get you off my back.

***

***
What a strange night that was!
It seemed so quiet, there on the hillside
- much more so than normal.
You could almost cut the silence with a knife.
And then those angels!
man! I thought we were done for!
- either that or going mad! -
But they were right
the babe was where they said.
Is this truly the Messiah?
But why should simple shepherds
be the first to know?

DESERTED WIFE

I won't be long,
he said,
four hours ago
and she had scarcely noticed
the banging
of the broken
wire door behind
him as he left,
the words of their anger
half-buried
in the dust of apathy.

I won't be long
he said
four weeks ago;
and now the strain
of hungry loneliness
had pulled
the once-soft flesh
tight across her face
while her heart fought
to find some reason
for the inevitable.

***

***

I won't be long
he said
four years ago,
but she scarcely remembers:
for time's
all-erasing hand
has blurred the days
together
and apathy returns.

AWAKENING

In my winter
like a rosebud, I
curled in upon myself
hidden
shielded
all my defences up:
till Your love came
spring-sun soft
and coaxed me to unfold
the petals of my spirit
to the warmth
of Your light.

NIGHT OF FRIGHT

palpable quiet
stifling night
atmosphere tight
tempers ignite
screaming fight
blood runs bright
flashing light
flee in fright
engulfed in night
deadly quiet

DON'T ASK ME TO BE YESTERDAY

Don't ask me to be yesterday.
Yesterday is dead; blown
away with evening's breeze
and buried with the setting sun.

Many moments' waves
have washed my life since then
and each
has taken something of me
with it
and left me
something of itself.
Many souls
have crossed the path of mine
and wandered with me
till our colours blended
and I see the world
in the light of them
and they in the light of me.

***

***

I am Now,
I am I:
yet not only I
for I am all that I
have ever known, and all
that I have ever done.

Neither ask me to be tomorrow.
Tomorrow is unborn:
her sunshine has not, yet,
lent warmth to bring to life
the seeds yet dormant in my soul;
nor can I know what furrows
tomorrow's rain will make
into the mountain of my being.

I am I,
I am Now.
Not yesterday
nor tomorrow,
but just this fleeting instant.
Don't ask me to be otherwise.

MORNING CITY FAR AWAY

Mist grey
against the bronze-gold dawn
dwarfed by distance
there the city stands
a sleeping ghost
like some
half-solid shadow
flung against the sky
a dream
wrapped in pink tissue
and waiting
for the opening of the day.

PETER

(Luke 5:1-11; John 21:7-14)

FISHERMAN
Cast on the other side,
He said,
although we had toiled all night
and our empty nets
and the rising sun
called it a futile thought.
But for Him we cast -
and the fish broke our nets
till I fell at His feet
in awe.
Come after Me and catch men,
He said,
and my fisherman's heart
lept for joy
as I thought of the fish
to be dragged from the depths
and laid at the Master's feet:
brought in at His word
by my strength and skill -
a catch so great
it would almost sink
the boats
of heaven itself.

***

***

Ah, yes!
I would fish for men
and bring to Him
a worthy prize
caught in the nets
which I, Peter, cast.

SHEPHERD
Cast on the other side,
He said,
and again our nets were full.
But I ran to Him
leaving the catch
for others to drag ashore.
Do you love Me,
He asked,
with knowing eyes
that melted my heart
and my soul:
and in their light I saw
      a fire
      a girl
      a question asked
      and my answer,
      I don't know the man!

                              ***

***

In the light of those eyes
how could I claim love?
I answered,
I'm fond of You, Lord.
And without hesitation
without condemnation
He said
Feed My sheep.
And my heart bowed in awe
as I thought of the sheep
with their hunger
their sorrow
their fears:
and my wounded heart knew
I would give my life
lest they, too, stumble
in that dark gulley
where I, Peter, fell.

WINTER HOPE

Like winter's golden dream
of spring;
like midnight thoughts
of daybreaks yet to come:
a dream unrealised yet,
a hope still to be born -
a golden whisper
half lost
in silence:
a daffodil in May.

(NB This poem was written in the Southern Hemisphere where winter is June to August.)

FOR BRIAN

A laughing, lisping age
- clap hands, fall down -
when tears are fierce
but in a moment gone,
and running is
the only pace you know.
An age
of miracles
when every day's discoveries
are new
and tomorrow
is a million years away.
A time
for chasing butterflies
- clap hands, fall down -
for blowing
dandelion clocks;
for mud pies
and bruised knees
and NOISE!
Such an enchanting age
is three.

THE HERMIT

I went to the hermit
on top of the hill,
saying, I seek for peace:
and he said, Go
to the battle's noise
to the clamour
and fear
and strife,
for only the peace
that can stand its strain
will stay with you
throughout your life.

I went to the hermit
on top of the hill
asking, Where shall I find joy?
and he said, Go.
First learn to weep,
let your heart be pierced
by life's thorns,
and amid your tears
find that ray of light
that cannot be doused
by life's storms.

***

***

I went to the hermit
on top of the hill
saying, I want to be free:
and he said, Go,
let yourself be chained
let them tie you foot and hand:
for the spirit that soars
from a dungeon cell
will never be bound by man.

I went to a Cross
on top of a hill
saying, Saviour, teach me to love.
And He said, Go
to the gutters and streets
to the lepers and beggars and whores,
then to those who will curse you
and spit in your face,
who will pierce your hands and your heart:
for the love that can stand
the stench and the filth,
that can love through the hatred and sneers,
the kind of love with which I have love you
will stand past a million years.

GOODBYE

Goodbye
is such a sad word
particularly
when it takes from me
one whose laughter
has danced on my own lips,
and whose tears
have flooded my own eyes.
Through hell and high water,
we said -
and, till today,
we faced them together.
You made me rich
with your wisdom
and your love,
and I
had hoped to make you rich
with mine.

***

***

But now
that sad, sad word
Goodbye
takes you from me ...
but even that word
cannot take
the treasure in my heart:
that joyful memory
that for this brief, delightful hour
you were my friend.

DAY BEFORE PENSION

Her purse is light,
holding only
that last precious dollar,
change from the gas bill -
due last week,
paid this morning,
for fear they'd cut her off.
Somehow
the money hasn't spread too well
this fortnight -
but tomorrow
another cheque will come,
and she
will pay the rent
and try, somehow, to stretch
each remaining cent
to do a dollar's work.
Meanwhile
there it is:
one hundred cents -
her worldly wealth
until the postie calls
tomorrow.

***

***

The fridge is empty:
more barren
even than her purse.
But she must eat tonight
and so
must Mr Tibbs -
dear, faithful Mr Tibbs
her sole companion
confidante
and care:
the canine apology
who warms her feet
and chews her shoes,
and listens
when nobody else has time.
One hundred cents:
not much!
Just barely enough
for some milk,
or a little meat,
for Tibbs.
For herself?
There's a biscuit or two
stashed away in a jar,
and a cup of weak tea
made with used-before leaves.
She'll make do.

LOOK AT CHRISTMAS

Look at the Christmas lights
shining so bright
and think of the Light that came
piercing the cloud
of a sin-shrouded world
dispelling the darkness
of sin, guilt, and shame
and lighting the path
to come home again.

Look at the tree
evergreen and alive
and think of the Life that came
laying aside
the eternal throne
born in a cattle shed
to die in pain
that we might be brought
to life again.

***

***

Look at the gifts
wrapped with loving care
and think of the Love that came
into a world
that received Him not
yet still His love He gave
Healing, forgiving,
calling us back:
back to the Father's heart again.

WHOM SHALL I FOLLOW?

(1 Corinthians 11:1)

Whom shall I follow, Lord?
What man shall lead
my stumbling footsteps
up the rocky mount?
Who shall go before me
trying first
that pathway rough and steep?
Whose light shall guide?
Whose love shall pause
to bind my broken feet?
For I would follow You
and yet
my human need
cries that You would be
incarnate again for me -
would take on flesh and blood
that these, my human eyes,
may see;
and voice
that I might hear
and not confuse.
Lord, give me one
whom following
I may but follow You.

***

***

Whom shall they follow, Lord?
These lost and lonely ones
who cry for light -
these ones whose night
has hid Your face?
Whose hands shall guide
these babes' stumbling feet
and feed
these hungry with
Your living bread?
Whose back shall bear
the burden of the day
for these, too weak?
Your face, Your hands, Your back
they cannot see:
but they see me.
Lord, so possess
this, my humanity,
that they may follow You
by following me.

THE DOLL

She had watched it
in the window
for many months past,
small freckled nose
pressed hard
against cold glass,
breath making misty
patterns on the pane
as round blue eyes
gazed lovingly, longingly,
at the object of her desire.
Her gaze caressed
soft pink folds of tulle
and finely featured face -
with eyes that cry! -
and soft blonde curls.
And every time
she glimpsed the first
evening star
or broke the wish bone
from the Sunday dinner
or dropped a coin
down some hoped-to-be-magical well
her heart held only
one wish

***

***

as her five-year-old mind
pictured the doll
with blonde hair
and a pretty pink dress
and eyes that cry.

And then
night of miracles!
amid
the Christmas morning shouts
small hands ripped
at wrappings and ribbons
so carefully tied
and small heart filled
with all the joy
that it could know
as she gasped
in the wonder of delight
then ran out shouting
Mummy, Mummy, look!
my wish came true!

WAITING

He sits on the step
his bare
ten year old legs
pulled up under his chin
waiting
while the Old Man and Her
have one more for the road
and the shadows grow longer
in the darkening street.
Waiting! Why wait?
Go smash some street lights
to fill in some time ...
anything's better
than sitting here waiting.

He stands in the street
leaning listlessly
against a poster-plastered fence:
no where to go
no money to go there.
The job queue was long
and he got there too late -
Maybe next time,
just wait.
Wait! Why wait?

***

***

Go steal a car
and go for a spin,
blow the last of the Dole
on a mess of cheap booze
or get stoned ...
anything's better
than standing around
just waiting.

He sprawls on a bench
in a litter-strewn park
the coat from the Salvos
pulled over his legs
the empty metho bottle
shattered
where he threw it
when the last drop was gone:
and he waits ...
for sleep,
for day,
for another drink,
for death.
Mostly for death.
What could be more desired
when all of life
has been spent
waiting?

GOD IS SO STUBBORN

God is so stubborn.
Much as I try
to force Him
He obstinately refuses
to be tidily folded
neatly encapsulated
correctly labelled
and fitted into
my little box
called theology.

***

***

Instead
He rudely insists
on bulging out
here
there
and everywhere -
Untidy!
and just
when I think
I have Him
all squashed in
and am ready
to tie the final bow
making it presentable
He bursts out
shatters my theology
and forces me
to my knees
in worship.

HARSH WORDS

Your words cut down
to that dark place
where pain lies buried
deep within
and rend
the flimsy fabric
of that tomb.
Pain rushes forth
an angry ghost
fattened yet again
by words
that fly between
till hurtful words have ceased;
and grows yet more replete
on the ice-thick silence
that follows.
And then
a token touch
a token word
and we go on:
nothing healed
nothing changed
and pain is buried
yet again.

OLD HOUSES

I love old houses
large and easy
mellowed with years
and life.
A little rough
around the edges
perhaps, but then
so am I.
New houses
make harsh demands
of stark and spartan modernness
- impossible to such as I -
and make one feel
a stranger
in one's own domain.
Old houses
ask nothing
save to be
and to remember.

AFTERMATH

The terror has passed.

Men wipe
reddened
blistered hands
'cross black
and sweaty brows,
their despairing
eyes searching
razed horizons.
The hopes
and aspirations
of the years
lie gutted;
charcoaled tombs
of lost labours.
Charred
stumps of trees
and fences
glow
with the mocking
taunting eyes
of the Destroyer,

***

***
and the air
is thick
with his breath.

Life alone remains:
but that
enough to clear
the rubble
and begin again.

DEFINING THE INFINITE

We seek to encase
Your picture
in our own misshapen frames:
we fashion
images of You
cast in our likeness
and allow them to become
cages
in which we would imprison You.

> (How can minds
> which cannot comprehend
> the earth on which we live
> lay hold of You
> who created the universe
> at Your will?
> How can we
> who cannot plumb the depths
> of the finite
> seek to reach the limits
> of infinity?)

***

***
We are too small
to simply stand in awe
and marvel:
rather
we would shrink You
seek to make You
smaller than ourselves
hold You
beneath our microscopes
and examine You
till You lie dead
on some dissecting table ...

FIRST LOVE

We ran together then -
crazy children
more in love
with love
than with each other:
our lives stretched
before us
      - a golden highway -
and our passionate
young legs were anxious
to eat up every mile.

We stood together then -
two lost
and lonely souls
battered by life,
hurt and rebellious:
together
we would fight the world
      - if only we hadn't
        lost ourselves
        in fighting each other!

                                                  ***

***

We looked in mirrors, then
seeing not
our hopeless differences
but only the warped
reflections of our own
wants
needs
desires.
Torn by forces
that ripped our bodies
and shredded our hearts
we surrendered
      - and dared to call it love.

CALVARY (Song)

Hour of triumph! Raise the cry
throughout the Heavens of victory!
For death, in seeking to destroy,
has spent itself at Calvary.

One Man has stood for all mankind
to know in full hell's agony -
the Son alone was pure enough
to pay the price of Calvary.

Freely He stepped into my place
to bear the burden meant for me;
freely He took my sin and death
and carried them to Calvary.

"It is finished!" rings the cry,
the victory-cry for man set free;
Justice and Love both satisfied
the task complete at Calvary.

No more the price is mine to pay,
no more the judgement mine to see:
I died, and rose again in Him,
my death destroyed at Calvary.

DEWDROP

Dewdrop quivers
poised
on blushing velvet petal,
like trembling teardrop
on baby cheek.
Precious, momentary thing
rolls down,
caressing petal-cheek,
and drops.

INCREDIBLE LOVE (Song)

Incredible love that gave me life
though knowing all that life would be
He saw my sin, He knew the price
that He must pay to set me free …
Incredible love!

Incredible love that gave me choice
though knowing I would not choose Him –
That did not falter but gave all
that He at last my love might win …
Incredible love!

Incredible love that gave up heaven
to walk with man upon the earth:
the God who made the universe
now comes as one of lowly birth …
Incredible love!

Incredible love that gave His life
to pay the price of sin for me
He bore my wounds, He bore my tears,
He bore my death at Calvary …
Incredible love!

***

***

Incredible love that gave me hope
when I was lost in darkest sin
He sought me out, He brought me home,
He set me free to worship Him …
Incredible love!

Incredible love that gave me all –
all heaven's riches spent on me –
filled me with life with joy with peace
for now and for eternity …
Incredible love!

THE DISPOSABLE MAN

Sitting alone
outside the world,
his mind flickers back
to the laughing
full days,
to the tears
and the work
and the love that he gave;
but
empty now
of the fullness he had
rusted by years
and battered by life
and no longer useful,
he's pushed aside -
thrown away like an old tin can:
the disposable man.

From his silent corner
his lonely eyes watch
for those he knows
won't come.

***

***

They grew fat
on his fullness
and tall
on his time,
but now
their own frantic fullness fills
their every hour:
the world has no time
for an old empty can -
less still for
the disposable man.

The grey shadows flit
through his greyer days
till night closes in
with welcome release,
and, horror! he's gone
and the world stops still
while they weep
for their loss
though for years unseen,
and somehow find
sandwiched in between
the hustle of yesterday
and the bustle of tomorrow
a few feet of ground
for an old tin can
and an hour - too late! -
for the disposable man.

THE SPIRIT OF XMAS

Deck the halls with boughs of holly -
I would
had not my house been flattened
by the bombs of a war
I do not understand
and do not want to.

Cut the cake and pass the pudding -
I would
were not my rice bowl empty
and my future filled
with an abundance of rice bowls
similarly barren.

Open gifts and snap the crackers -
I would
were not my time so filled
in scratching an existence
from a land which gives no gifts
save early death.

***

***

Dance for joy and sing sweet carols -
I would
but you would find my ragged clothes
unfit for your festivities
and joy is a commodity
I've never known.

So celebrate your Saturnalia -
eat, drink and be merry -
but tell me not of One
who, being full, emptied Himself:
I see it not in you.

THE OFFERING

You brought me a flower:
offered it
half crushed
in grubby hands
and smiled
shyly bold
your brown eyes fixed on mine.
And then,
the moment gone,
you ran back
to your cars
in the dirt
leaving me
to keep
the flower of
this moment in my heart.

LIKE SWEETEST GRAPES (Song)

Like sweetest grapes from off the vine,
choice olives gathered from the bough,
and crushed to make the finest wine
and oil, oh let me offer now
my life, as a libation poured
upon the altar of my Lord.

Stopping not to count the cost
nor question reckless love like this
break now the alabaster box:
break now my heart as He broke His.
As rarest perfume, richly sweet
just pour me out at Jesus' feet.

As freely as the crimson tide
that flowed to cleanse my scarlet sin:
the blood and water from His side
that fount of love from deep within -
oh, let me, to see others freed
be so poured out to meet their need.

GEORGE

Lost
amid a chaos of cars
a sea of parts
and tools and grease
hard, at first, to see -
like an animal
camouflaged
and blending perfectly
with its habitat,
its natural home.
He comes
pulling himself out
from his surroundings
a wiry little man
full of years
and gentleness,
twinkling eyes
that speak not
of many sorrows past,
but only of the joy
the sheer adventure
of the now.

***

***

A misplaced leprechaun
speaking fondly
of his wife
his kids
and theirs
and a thousand
every day things
touched by his magic
and made special.
Retire?
Foolish thought!
Retirement is for the old
and while
a car
a spanner
and a willing ear remain
he never will grow old.

FOR ME

How can I say thank you
to One who
laying aside omnipotence
became powerless -
for me?
who laying aside omniscience
chose to know nothing -
for me?
who laying aside infinity
chose the confines
of frail humanity -
for me?
who left behind the worship
of a hundred million angels
and chose insignificance -
for me?
How do I say thank you
to One who chose
rejection
loneliness
misunderstanding
contempt
and betrayal -
for me?

***

***

to One who gave His back
to the lashes I deserved?
whose hands and feet
were skewered
by fierce iron spikes
forged from my sin?
How do I say thank you
to One who chose to hang
naked before the world
His sinlessness polluted
by the sewerage
of my sin?
A million thank yous
could not suffice.
What shall I give You?
All I am
all I have
all I can ever be
my every right
my every desire
together
are less than dust
on the scales of such love
but all are Yours.
Lord, let me only be
Your bondslave.

ASK NOT

Ask not
who am I?
nor, what?
for every who
is but a wall
and every what
an iron bar to build
a prison
a solid boundary
beyond which "I"
may not pass:
till the walls are mistaken
for that which they enclose
and all within
for emptiness.
Rather
strip yourself
of every who
and what
until at last
you are content to stand
naked and unashamed
and simply say,
I am.

MARC

Golden curls and huge
heart-melting eyes
fringed with black;
fawn-soft freckles
scattered across
up-turned nose
and laughing, round cheeks ...
    ... and angel or a rascal?
Warm, wet kisses
and pudgy, still-dimpled
baby hands in mine;
whispered secrets
and incredible stories;
temper tantrums and tears
and then
arms outstretched
for forgiveness;
pigeon-toed walk
and waddling run ...
    ... my angel
      my rascal
      my son.

FULL CIRCLE

A child
with dirty, twisted hands
reached out to mine
tried, once,
to touch me with
soul-sad eyes
that begged my love:
and I,
Fool!
imagining that this
was mine,
would give it not.

A man
bound in chains
of fire-filled steel
cried to me,
once,
and begged my peace:
and I,
Fool!
fearing for its loss
would share it not.

***

***
Where,
now,
that love that I
kept locked so
safely in my
heart?
Where
that peace
I hugged so closely
to my bosom?

I turn
full circle.
I,
the crippled child;
I,
the fettered man,
reach out to You
and beg of You
Your love, Your peace:
and You,
God!
knowing these are Yours,
give freely.

DECISION

O soul!
Would there were but
one path to tread
one course to steer
marked clear
upon my chart.
Or if there must be two
would one were lit
with bright
and flashing signs
with golden arrows
and a guiding star.
Would I could clearly see,
from here,
the end of each;
could stand above
my earthbound place and scan
their routes; could know
the lurking dangers
hid along each way ...

***

***
But no.
I stand instead
between two strange
and yet untravelled paths;
my vacillating spirit
searching
for some guiding clue.
There is no retreat:
one road leads to
my destiny
the other
to damnation -
and I,
alone,
must choose ...
     which?

JULY MORNING

Early morning
dark-light beckons;
the roaring
whispering sea
calls me;
and the salt-smell
tang in my nostrils
draws me
like some
magnetic and mystical
perfume.

(I rise slowly:
warm blankets
have a special pull
that challenges even magic.)

But the call
of fading
night is stronger:
draws me out,
then slaps
my face with ice-
solid air.

***

***

My toes plough
into sand
soft and sinking
as snow, but not
as cold;
legs move
in rhythm with
the surging sea.

There is no
horizon.
Mist hangs
from sky to sea
blotting out
that world-made line
between time
and eternity:
and I
could walk forever
to infinity.

NO GOD?

(Psalms 14:1 "The fool says in his heart 'There is no God'.")

No God?
Though countless blazing spheres
stud endless space
on nothing hung,
and secret glories hide
where man will never see?

No God?
Though life in multitudinous forms
bursts ceaselessly from earth
and in all its needs
meets function apt for it?

No God?
Though unessential beauty
the universe pervades
and fools
have mind enough
to doubt their own reality?

***

***

Is it not, rather,
No! God!
No! I will not bow!
No! I will not serve!
No! I will not obey!
No! I will not believe!
For belief demands surrender:
No! God!

AN END

I touch you
      share your world
           but you don't know me.
My nights
      and my days are lived for you
           but you have no time for me.
I wait
      hoping
           eager for your return:
but your thoughts
      your life
are in the world you have left,
to which you will return tomorrow.

I dream
      my dreams alone
           not daring to bother you with them;
and cry
      my tears in solitude
           for you cannot understand.
You have forgotten
      - or did you ever know? -
           how to share the unimportant things;
till love has died
buried in the contemptuous coals of familiarity:
           and what is left?

GALATIANS 2:20

You forced me to this:
dragged me to it
kicking and screaming
all the way ...
hauled me before
Your judgement-mercy seat
Your tree of death
and sentenced me
to Your life.

You drew me to this;
wooed me to it
yearning and longing
aching to be done
with that vile clinging death
I once called life.
I cry for fullness
and You in mercy give
a still more aching emptiness
that yearns for death
till I embrace
Your tree of death-made-life
and dying live
self
impaled.

FIVE LOAVES

Just five loaves -
Lord, what are they
when thousands faint with hunger
all about?
Five small loaves -
Lord, they would barely
meet the need
of one.
For five thousand?
Shall we give
to each a crumb?
Five useless loaves!
        Yet You took:
        and their smallness
        vanished
        in Your infinity;
        You blessed
        speaking words of power,
        bringing change;
        You broke:
        cracked their crusty shell
        and tore apart
        their comfortable roundness;
        You gave
        and multitudes received
        more than enough.   ***

***
Just one life -
Lord, what is it
to millions crying
       dying
every day?
One small, ordinary life -
can this life make
a mark on even one?
One useless life!

              Lord, take
                    bless
                          break
                                and give
            this life
            no longer insignificant
            but multiplied
                    by all You are.

SURRENDER

Through a thousand
sleepless nights You hunt me;
across ten thousand
bleak and dreary days stalk me
Your desperate, lonely prey.
Down every corridor
of my soul you follow me
till even in my own
heart is no hiding place
and my mind can find no shadow
to blot out Your light.
Why
do You hunt me?
I am
no prize game!
Better far than I
are to be had -
go after them!
Yet still You pace me
down the hallways of eternity:
still shadow me
through every half-hopeful
escape;
till now I lie
beaten, cornered:

***

***

trapped!
Till the darkness
of my light
surrenders to the light
of Your darkness,
and the clamour
of my soul is stilled,
obedient only
to the silent Voice
that shouts,
Be still
and know that I am God.

DESOLATION

I stand alone
on my desolate
wind-whipped pinnacle
reaching out to skies
that have retreated
into the darkness of infinity
and longing
for the warm soil
that has frozen and
fallen away beneath me
till there is only
this bare rock
and I.

My skin burns
for the touch of dew
and evening's breeze
and I hunger
for the scent of sea air
and the taste
of your morning kiss -
but these
are dim and fading memories
(or maybe dreams)
and this bare rock
is I.

JACK

The dulling words dropped,
lead-like, on my heart,
that told me you were dead.
My tear-blurred eyes still see
your charcoal face;
ears hear the floating strands
of music that so filled your world.
Your hands wrought magic;
your unlearned wisdom was
too deep for books.
Now all is gone.
Yet, in our hearts, you live:
and immortality is partly this,
that love remains.

NATURE'S TRIUMPH

Hot wind that whispers, aching
cross a thousand acre sea
of death; and life
that clutching clings to hell's
last held-out hope
at withered waterhole and cracked
creek bed.
Gone grass, gone green, gone grain!
And rain,
forgotten word
of some lost language, now
like all the world to sight and mind,
shrivelled, lost.
Singed sky the white-hot dome
of wilted world made red
with dust and death;
and heat's relentless hand
that crushes all
and writes in the remains,
"Here man is not supreme!"

FAREWELL

(For a departing class)

Farewell!
One word
yet worth a hundred thousand
words, tears, smiles and memories:
to the departing soldier
a lifetime
wrapped, and perhaps soon
to be sealed forever;
to the returning traveller
laughter
a mind stocked full of pictures
and a pledged return.
To you, who leave us now,
a hundred hands of friendship,
a thousand days of laughter
and many streams of tears;
success and failure,
hope
and, sometimes, near despair;
and, most of all,
our prayer for each of you:
a future in which you will
fare well.

SUBSTITUTE

It should have been I
in the judgement hall
facing the charges brought:
indicted justly for my wrongs
before a righteous Judge.
Yet You stood, instead,
the sinless God
hauled for judgement
before sinful man.
You spoke not
to defend Your innocence
but in silence bore my guilt
and in my place
received the sentence due to me.

It should have been I
whose back was whipped
for beatings
are for the backs of fools,
and I in foolishness
have set before You other gods
of stone, of flesh, of thought,
but mostly of myself,
whilst You
wisdom personified
have brought the truth. ***

***

It should have been I
whose hands and feet were nailed
to cruel beams
wrenched
as they shuddered into place
and torn
by the weight of sin's burden.
For my hands
have often been
the instrument of evil
and yet more often still have failed
to do the good they could have wrought;
my feet have carried me
to places where Your Spirit
could not comfortably rest.
But your hands
brought only life
and Your feet
led you only in the Father's paths.

It should have been I
whose head was crowned with angry thorns
for thoughts of anger
hatred, envy, lust and greed
are not strangers to its paths
and my mind
in rebellion
has often sought
to raise itself above the throne of God.

***

***

But Your mind bowed
before the Father's will
obedient even
to this ignominious end.

It should have been I
whose heart was pierced
this heart in which
the depths of degradation lurk;
whose motives all
are tainted with corruption
and whose purest thoughts
stink of death.
Instead, Your heart of love
was rent
not by the soldier's sword
but by my guilt.

It should have been I
who died
exposed in naked shame
before the eyes of all
who cared to look;
screaming eternally
to unresponding infinity
for the just God
who turned His head away.

***

***

But You,
the righteous One
received my wages due
and I
walking free and clean
offer my inadequate response:
Thank You.
Thank you.

THE PHOTO

Who were you?
Once-pretty face
faded by years.
Laughing sad eyes
hold secrets
once open
long since buried.
What dreams
what plans
what visions
bore that spirit
soaring
through the
yet-to-be?
What fears
what uncertainties
pulled it back
pinioned
to the now-is
and the once-was?
What joys
moved you
to laughter?
What sorrows
to tears?

***

***
Try as I might
I cannot put
this old head
on those
young shoulders.
I knew you,
once,
but time's
relentless tide
has washed
your footprints
from my mind's sand.
I was you,
once,
but now
we are strangers.

NOT A POEM

write a poem
they said
i dont
know how to
write a poem
i said
its easy
just write a paragraph
in prose
then chop it up into
lines of varying
length
she said
oh and dont forget
to strip out all the
punctuation
she said
so I did
and now
she says
this is a poem
but i am not happy
i know that strict meter
is not necessary

***

***

but surely a poem
should have rhythm
cadence
surely it should sing
and i understand
it doesnt have to rhyme
but surely to rhyme
and not slip into
doggerel
is the greater skill
i want the greater skill
i want poetry
that sings
and dances
verbal music
not a haphazard collection
of words
strewn on paper
like a two year olds blocks
toppled
on the floor

some people say
this is a poem
i am not one of them

but then
i could be wrong

BY JESUS' BLOOD (Song)

By Jesus' blood I have been saved
By Jesus' blood alone:
He has me lifted from the grave
And brought me to His throne.

No act of mine could merit such
a loving sacrifice
That He, my God, love me so much
To pay the Cross's price.

How can I love You, loving King,
When my heart is so small?
I am a weak and helpless thing
and You are all in all.

Lord, stretch my heart to know Your love
And fill my soul with praise
That I may shout Your truth above
The world's mad noisy ways.

I will through life Your servant be,
Joyful throughout my days,
and when death's light shall dawn on me
My soul shall be Your slave.

SURE OF CHRIST'S LOVE (Song)

I am sure of Christ's love for me
Love that took Him to Calvary
Love that nailed Him upon the tree
Yes I'm sure, I'm sure
I'm sure of Christ's love for me.

I am sure of Christ's love for me
Love that lifted and set me free
Love that saved me eternally
Yes I'm sure, I'm sure
I'm sure of Christ's love for me.

I am sure of Christ's love for me
When I'm tossed on life's stormy sea
He's always waiting to comfort me
Yes I'm sure, I'm sure
I'm sure of Christ's love for me.

I am sure of Christ's love for me
When of this flesh He sets me free
Then into heaven He'll welcome me
Yes I'm sure, I'm sure
I'm sure of Christ's love for me.

LOST

Not this way.

These vistas evoke
no memory
no sweet familiar
scents or sounds
extend their hope
to stir remembrance.

This place is alien.
Perils
sensed not seen
lurk at every step.
A thousand grasping
fingers
stretch to strip
my flesh;
ten thousand twining
tendrils
steal out to trip
my feet.
Gall rises.

***

***

Sneering shadows swirl
seeping through
my skull
cavorting in their
death dance in
my brain;
horizons draw in
their thread
gathered by
spectral hands
and tighten about
my throat.

I have come
too far.
There is no
return.
I cower in
surrender.

INCARNATE

Infinity
compressed to human skin
growing
where growth was
never needed.

Eternity
confined in time
moving
past present future
irreversible
when all points
had been now.

Omnipotence
reduced to weakness
helpless
dependent

Omnipresence
tied to three dimensions
locked
in the limitation
of finite space

***

***

Omniscience
embraces amnesia
a blank slate
for creation to write upon

The universe's King
steps down to servanthood
humbled unto death
emptied willingly

HOUR OF TRIUMPH (Song)

Hour of triumph! Raise the cry
throughout the heavens of victory
for death in seeking to destroy
has spent itself at Calvary.

One Man has stood for all mankind
to know in full hell's agony -
the Son alone was pure enough
to pay the price of Calvary.

Freely He stepped into my place
to bear the burden meant for me
freely He took my sin and death
and carried it to Calvary.

"It is finished!" rings the cry
the victory-cry for man set free
Justice and Love both satisfied
the task complete on Calvary.

No more the price is mine to pay
no more the judgment mine to see:
I died, and rose again in Him,
my death destroyed at Calvary.

O LORD YOU STAND ALONE (Song)

O Lord You stand alone
alone You made the universe
You need no other gods
to make up what You lack.
And though the world
in all its foolishness
bows before many gods,
You alone I seek.

Take every other god from me
smash down every altar
let me stand unencumbered
before Your throne.
Take every other god from me
smash down every altar
That I may bring my offering
to You alone.

***

***

O Lord You stand alone
alone You rule the universe
and I would have You rule
likewise in my heart.
Every altar I have built
in all my foolishness
to worship other gods,
I now would tear it down.

From every other god I flee
smash down every altar
I will stand unencumbered
before Your throne
From every other god I flee
smash down every altar
that I may bring my offering
my whole self, my offering
an acceptable offering
                    to You alone.

WAR IN HEAVEN

The ancient battle lines have now been drawn.
No more this occupation will be borne.
The saints' accuser vile
Permitted for a while
Now from Jehovah's presence shall be thrown.

Michael, Prince of angels, stands to fight.
The enemy responds with all his might.
But victory has been planned
Since ever time began
For darkness has no power over light.

The Blood that seals this battle has been shed
Not by this army's body, but its Head
God's spotless lamb was given
His flesh by man's sin riven
Man's life by His redeemed now from the dead.

Through years the store of potent swords has grown -
The words and lives of those who are His own
Bought back from death's dark hold
In witness fiercely bold
With Him their lives in battle gladly sown.

***

***

Now at last the triumph has been sealed.
Impotent, the enemy must yield.
Hurled down from his place
Now against the race
of man, enraged, his fury he will wield.

Open fully now the heavens stand
No longer now is God shut off from man.
Those who would grasp God's power
Are free in this last hour
To rise in His authority and take the land.

BEYOND IMAGINATION

Imagine the cost:
heaven's perfection forsaken,
earth's corruption embraced;
infinity reduced
to a single cell;
omnipotence exchanged
for impotence;
omniscience buried
in ignorance.

Imagine the ache:
to walk in a world
that sees not,
nor cares;
revelation met
with rejection
and miracles
with scorn;
offering the eternal
to those who
only want a feed.

***

***

Imagine the agony:
flesh rent
stripped from bone;
nerves and tendons
cleft by spikes;
heart crushed.

Imagine the horror:
upon the sinless head
earth's sin-sewage
dumped;
the Father
turned away;
alone, forsaken.

Imagine the victory:
grave's doors
flung wide;
death's hold
shattered;
sin's power
forever smashed.

Imagine the wonder:
it was for me.

MEET THE AUTHOR

Lynn Fowler can't remember a time when she did not write. Her father was a creative writer and poet, so writing was part of her DNA.

Throughout a stormy childhood, adolescence and young adulthood she often retreated to poetry as a means of expressing what was in her heart, and a number of those poems were published in various magazines.

After becoming a Christian in her mid-twenties, Lynn was called into ministry, and much of her writing from that point forward reflected her relationship with the Lord Jesus Christ.

Lynn has two adult sons and five grandchildren. She lives alone in a tiny country town in Victoria, Australia, and divides her work time between ministry and writing. Her hobbies and interests include reading, knitting, cooking, art and building web sites.

www.ingramcontent.com/pod-product-compliance
Lightning Source LLC
Chambersburg PA
CBHW072211070526
44585CB00015B/1293